A BOOK OF BIG BUGS

by
Haris Petie

Prentice-Hall, Inc.,
Englewood Cliffs, New Jersey

Copyright © 1977 by Haris Petie

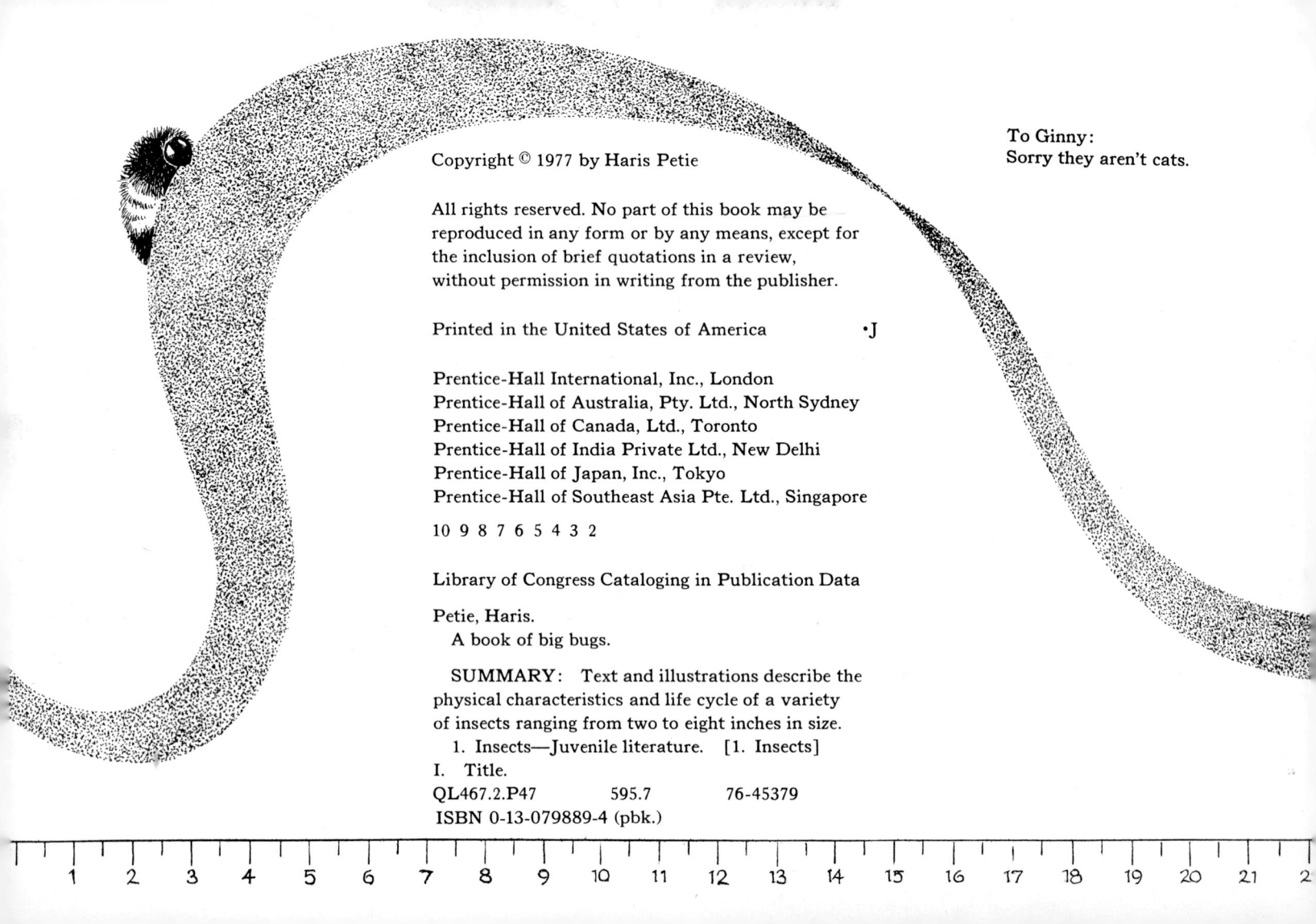

All rights reserved. No part of this book may be reproduced in any form or by any means, except for the inclusion of brief quotations in a review, without permission in writing from the publisher.

Printed in the United States of America

Prentice-Hall International, Inc., London
Prentice-Hall of Australia, Pty. Ltd., North Sydney
Prentice-Hall of Canada, Ltd., Toronto
Prentice-Hall of India Private Ltd., New Delhi
Prentice-Hall of Japan, Inc., Tokyo
Prentice-Hall of Southeast Asia Pte. Ltd., Singapore

10 9 8 7 6 5 4 3 2

Library of Congress Cataloging in Publication Data

Petie, Haris.
  A book of big bugs.

  SUMMARY: Text and illustrations describe the physical characteristics and life cycle of a variety of insects ranging from two to eight inches in size.
    1. Insects—Juvenile literature. [1. Insects] I. Title.
QL467.2.P47   595.7   76-45379
ISBN 0-13-079889-4 (pbk.)

To Ginny:
Sorry they aren't cats.

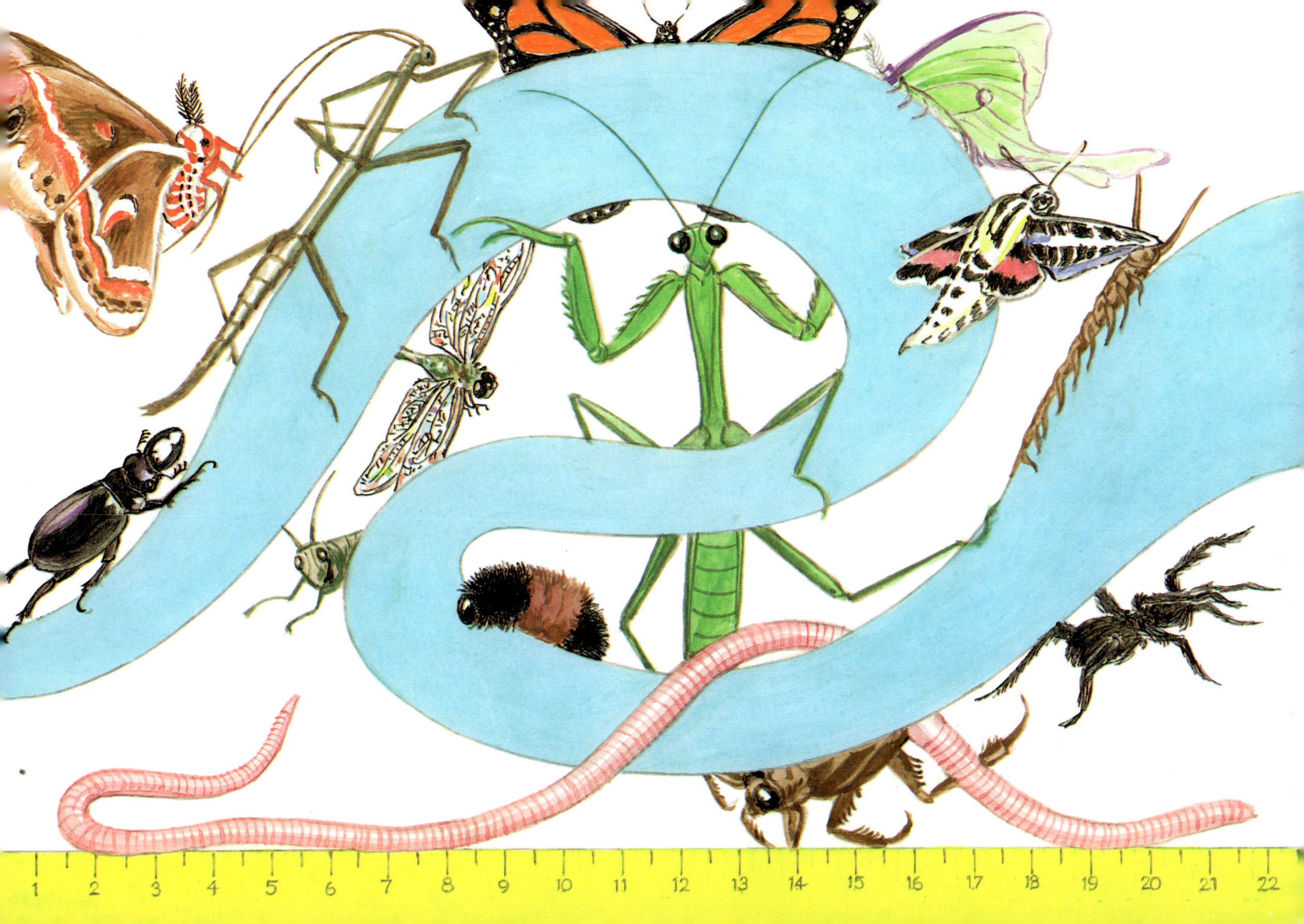
1 2 3 4 5 6 7 8 9 10 11 12 13 14 15 16 17 18 19 20 21 22

WOOLLY BEARS (5 CM)

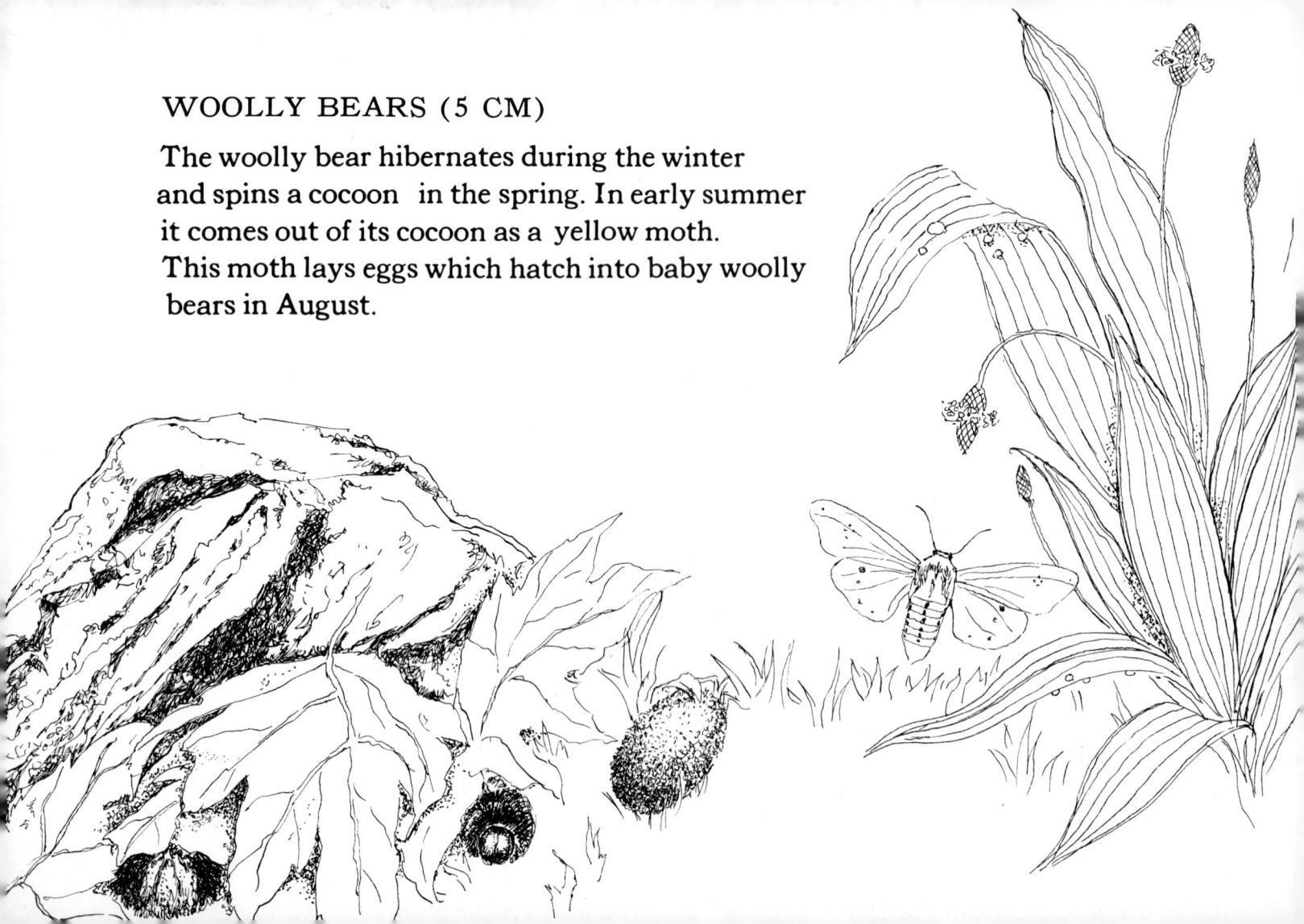

The woolly bear hibernates during the winter and spins a cocoon in the spring. In early summer it comes out of its cocoon as a yellow moth. This moth lays eggs which hatch into baby woolly bears in August.

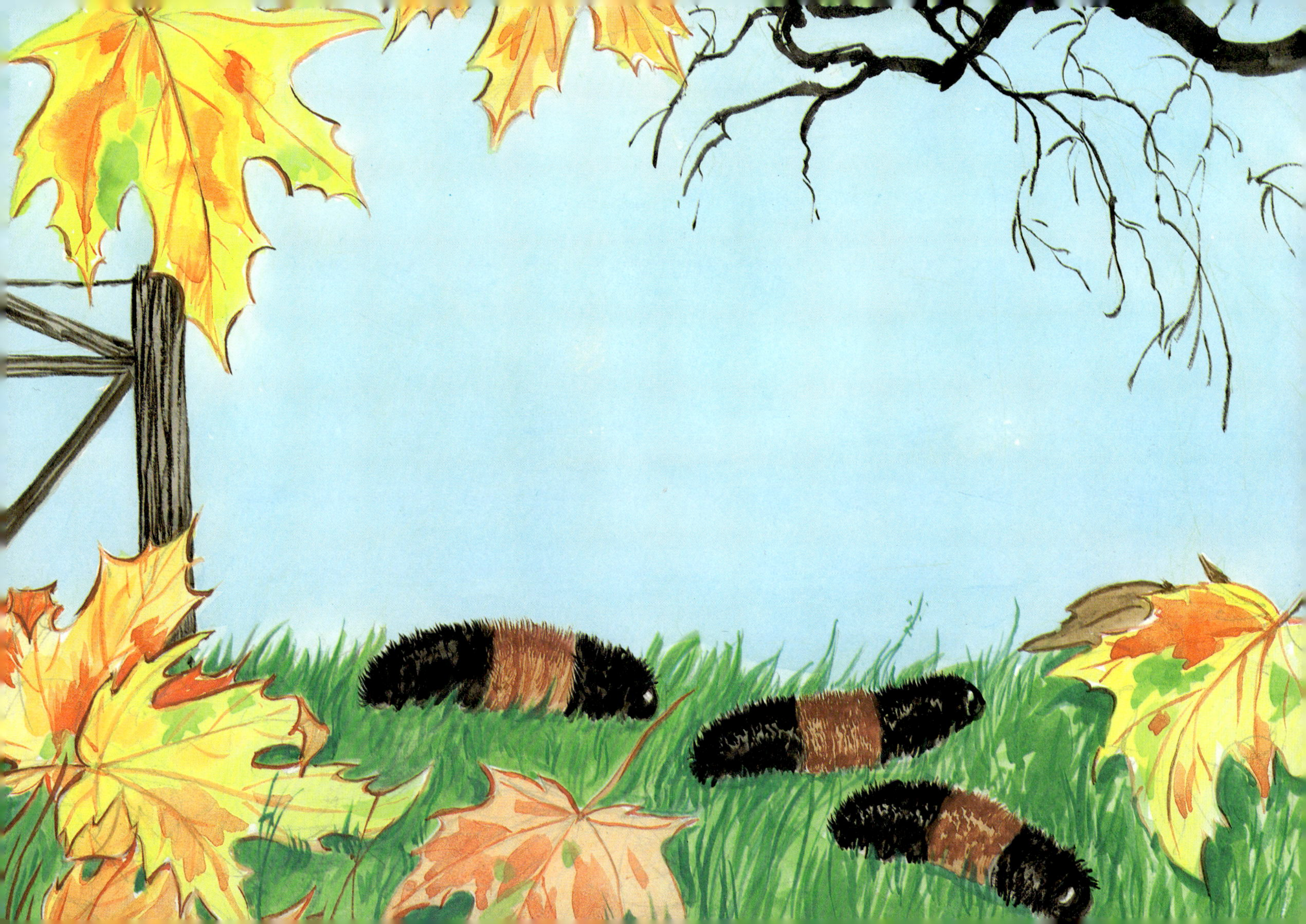

GRASSHOPPERS (5 CM)

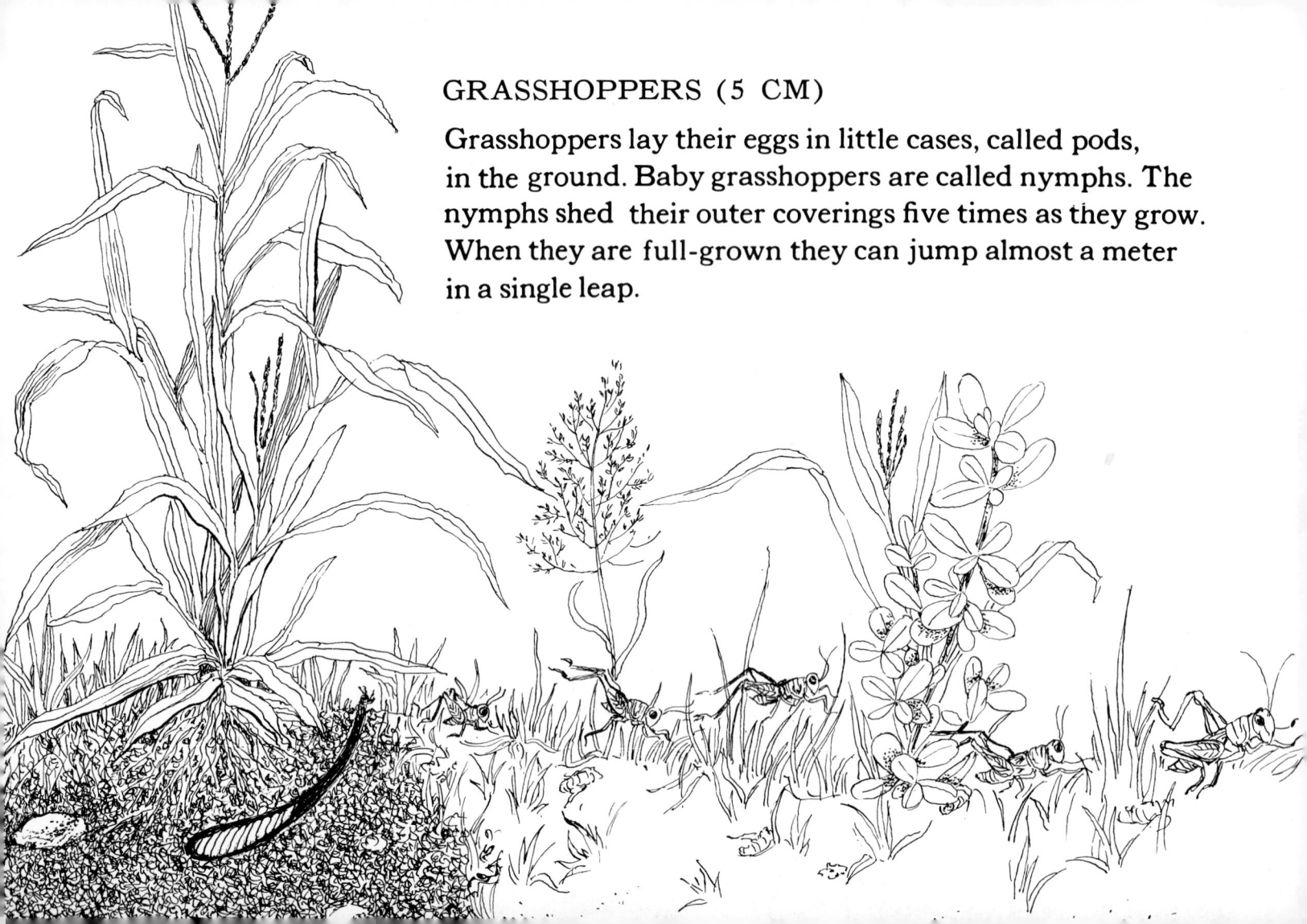

Grasshoppers lay their eggs in little cases, called pods, in the ground. Baby grasshoppers are called nymphs. The nymphs shed their outer coverings five times as they grow. When they are full-grown they can jump almost a meter in a single leap.

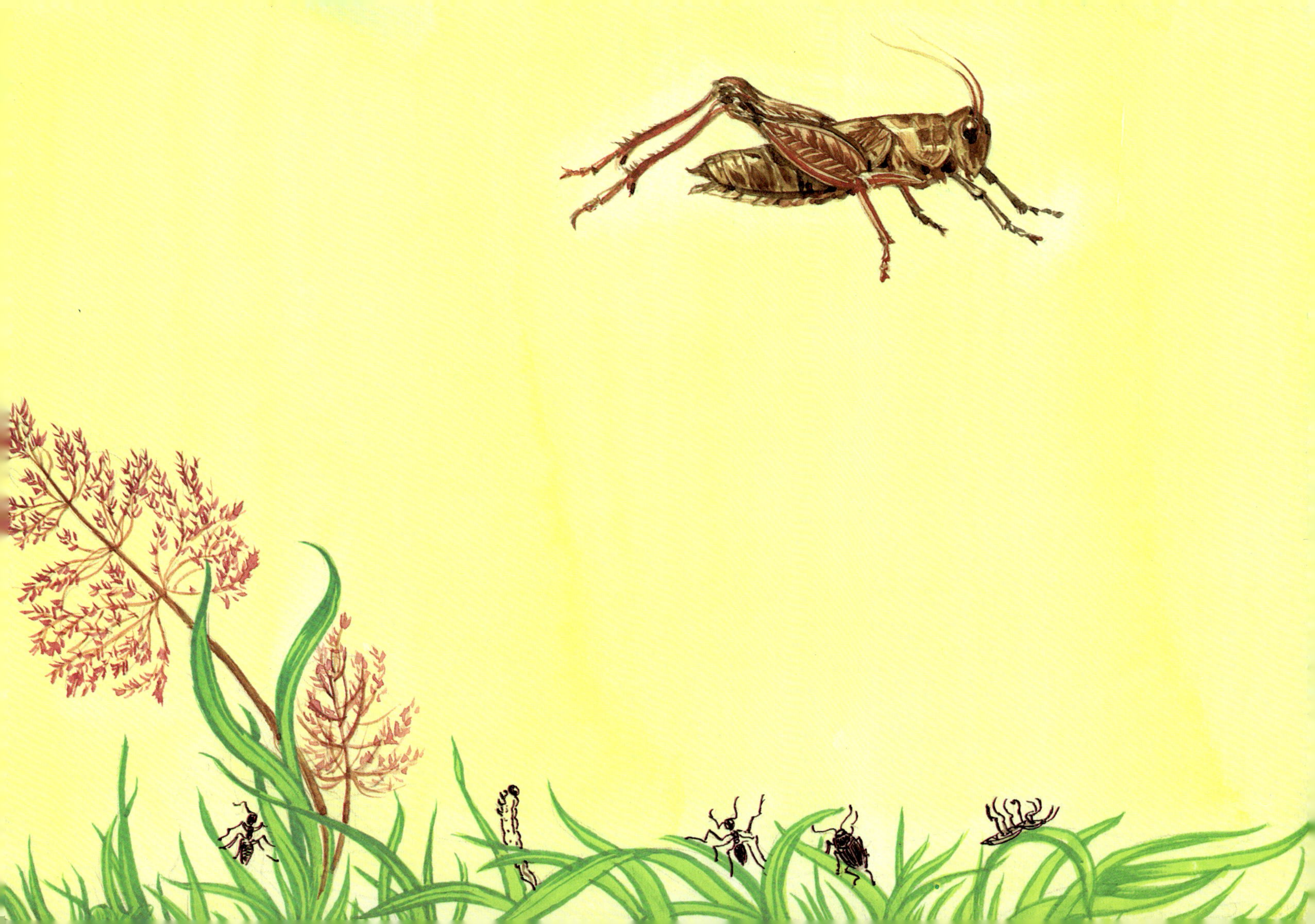

GIANT WATERBUG (6 CM)

Waterbugs live in quiet ponds. The mother waterbug lays her eggs on the father waterbug's back. He carries them until they hatch. Then the babies fall off and swim away.

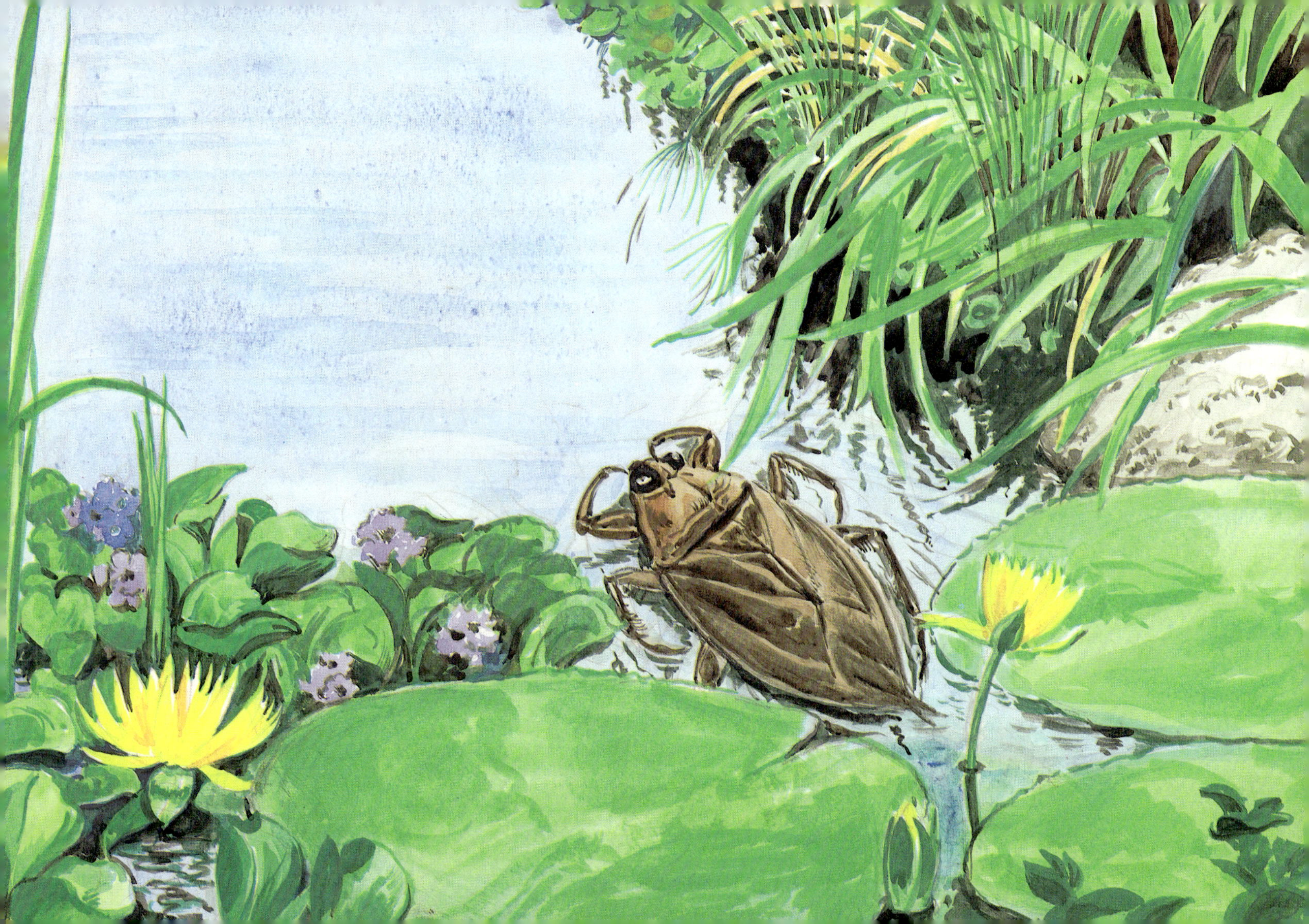

STAG BEETLE (7½ CM)

Stag beetles lay their eggs in hollow trees. The baby beetles are called grubs. They eat dead wood and leaves that they find on the ground. It takes the grubs over a year to grow to full size.

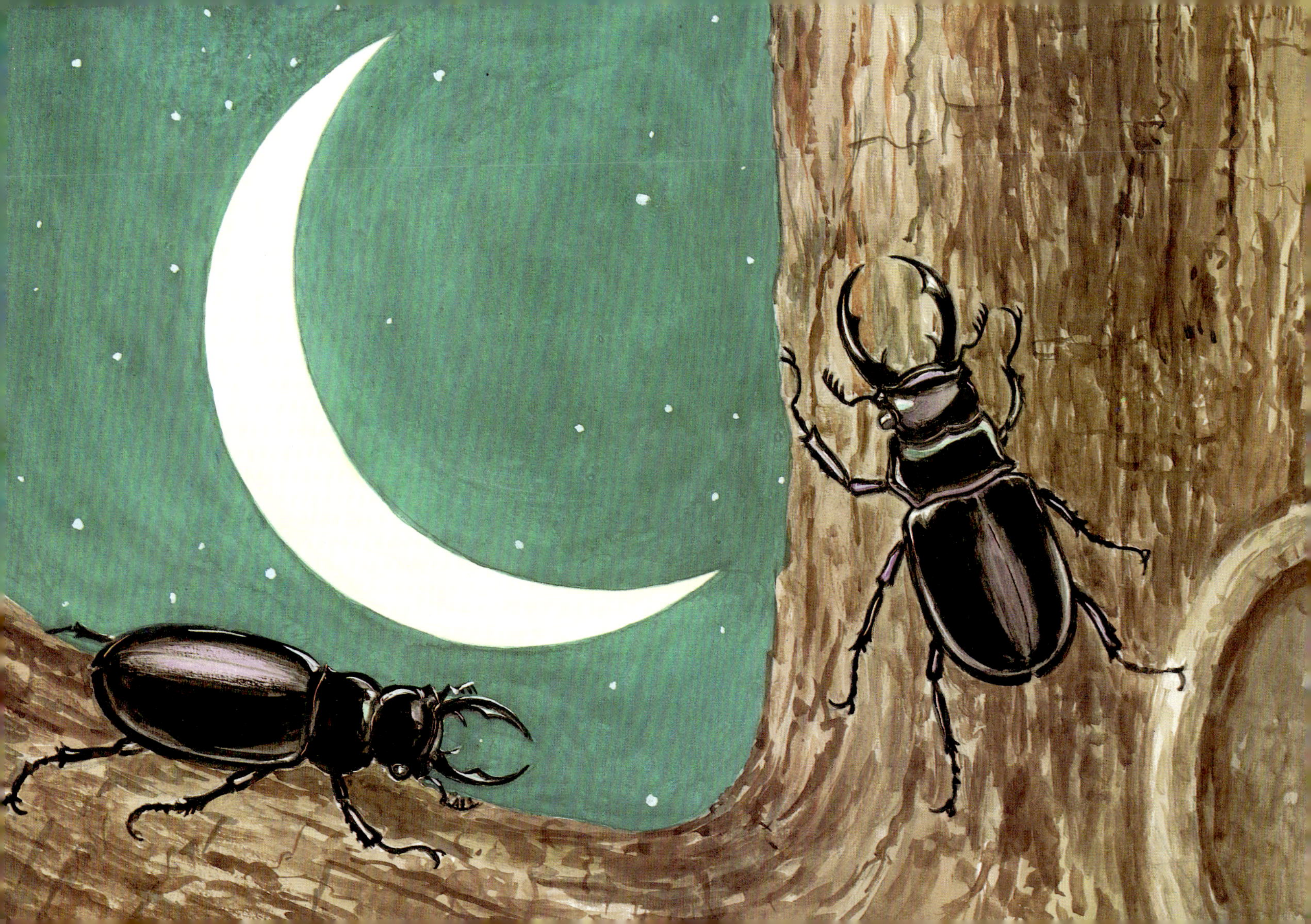

LUNA MOTH (9 CM)

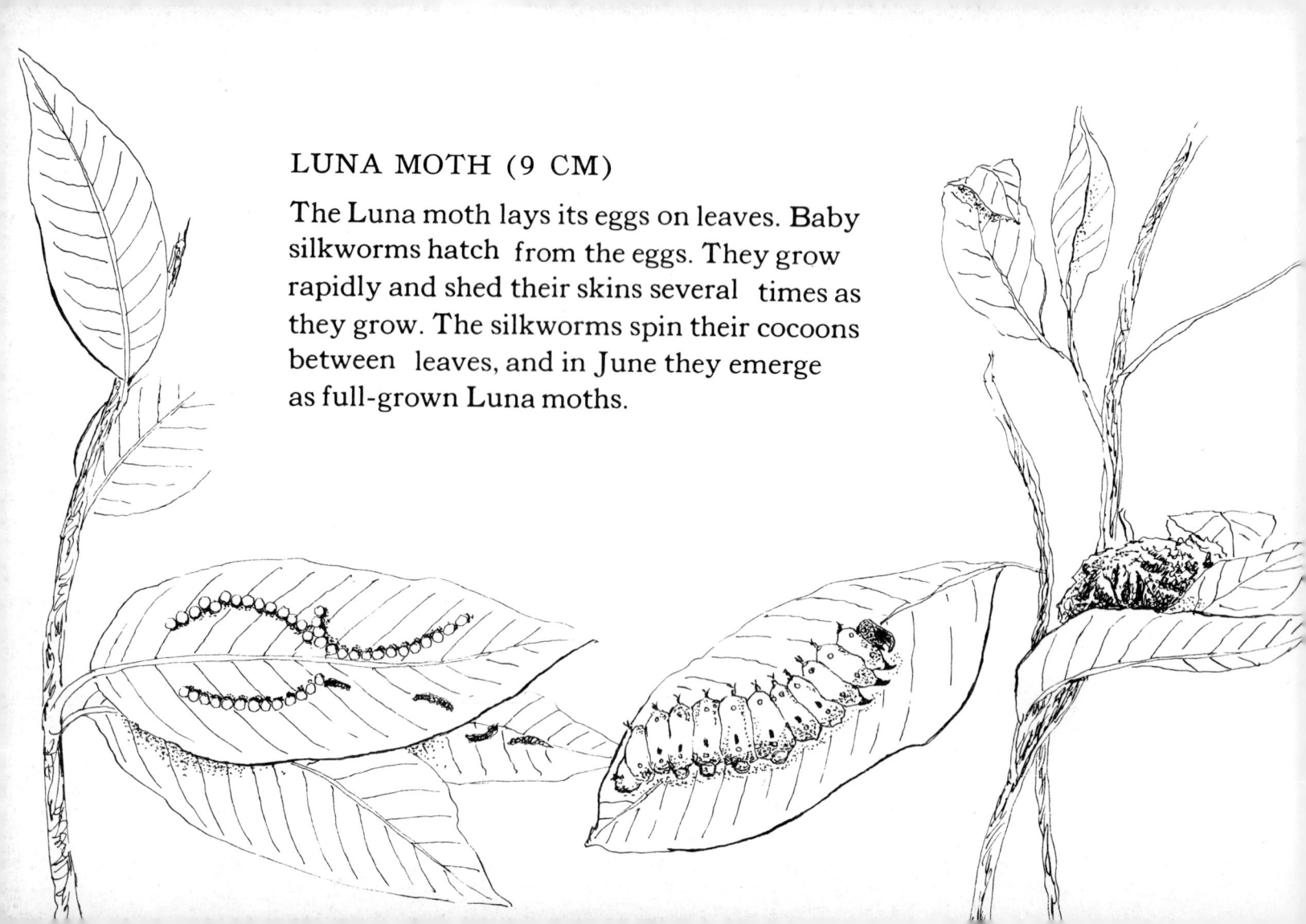

The Luna moth lays its eggs on leaves. Baby silkworms hatch from the eggs. They grow rapidly and shed their skins several times as they grow. The silkworms spin their cocoons between leaves, and in June they emerge as full-grown Luna moths.

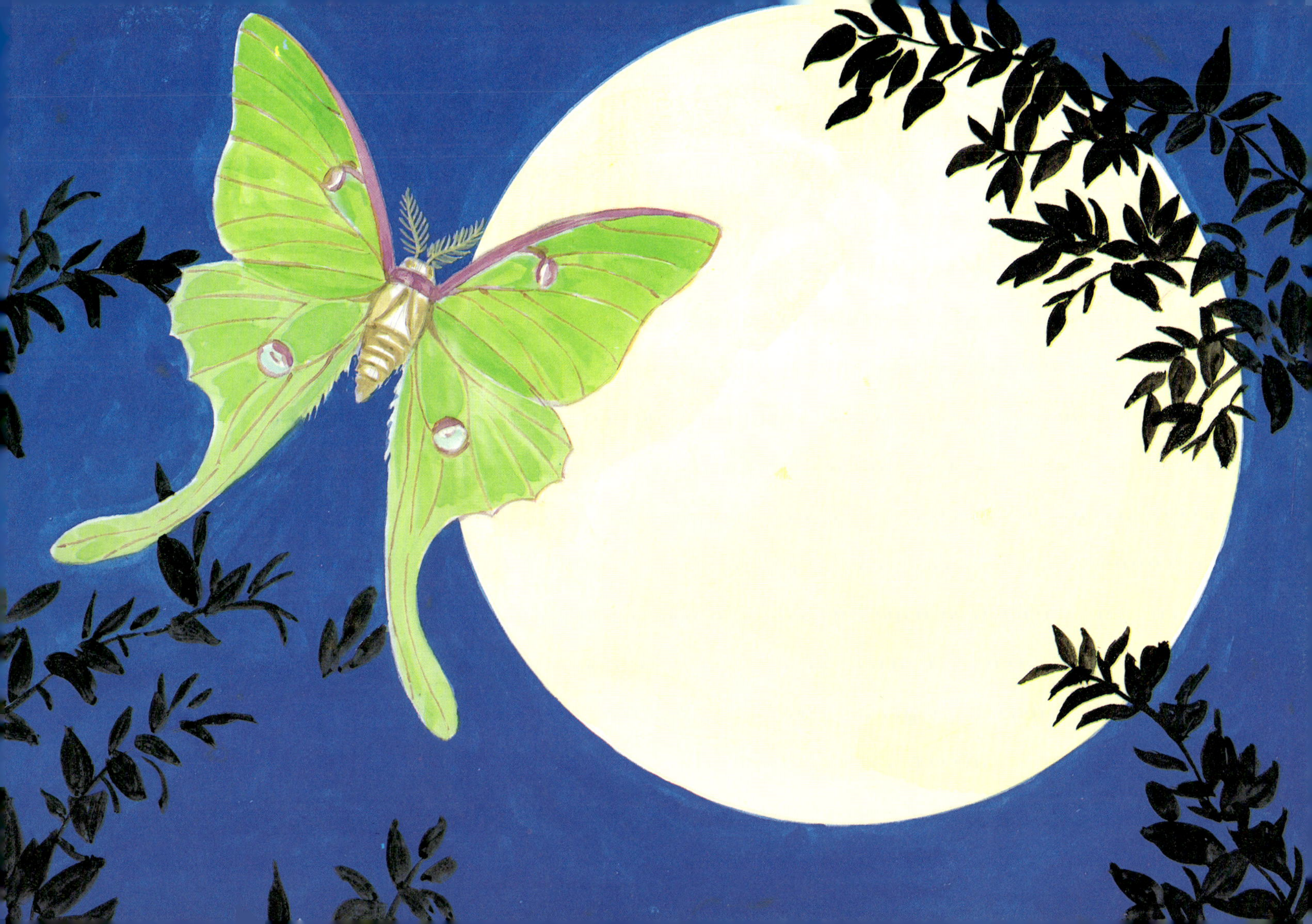

SPHINX MOTH (10 CM)

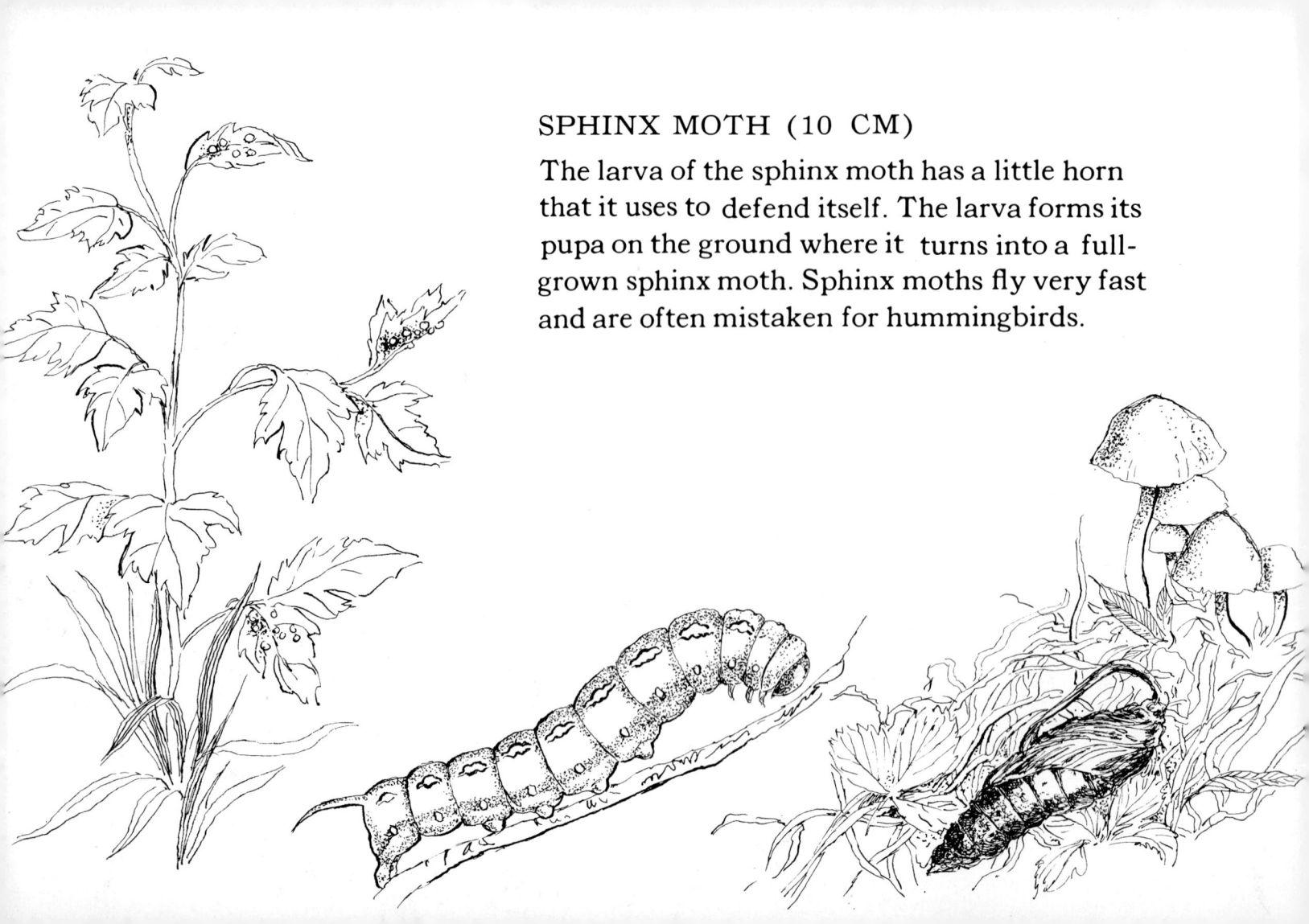

The larva of the sphinx moth has a little horn that it uses to defend itself. The larva forms its pupa on the ground where it turns into a full-grown sphinx moth. Sphinx moths fly very fast and are often mistaken for hummingbirds.

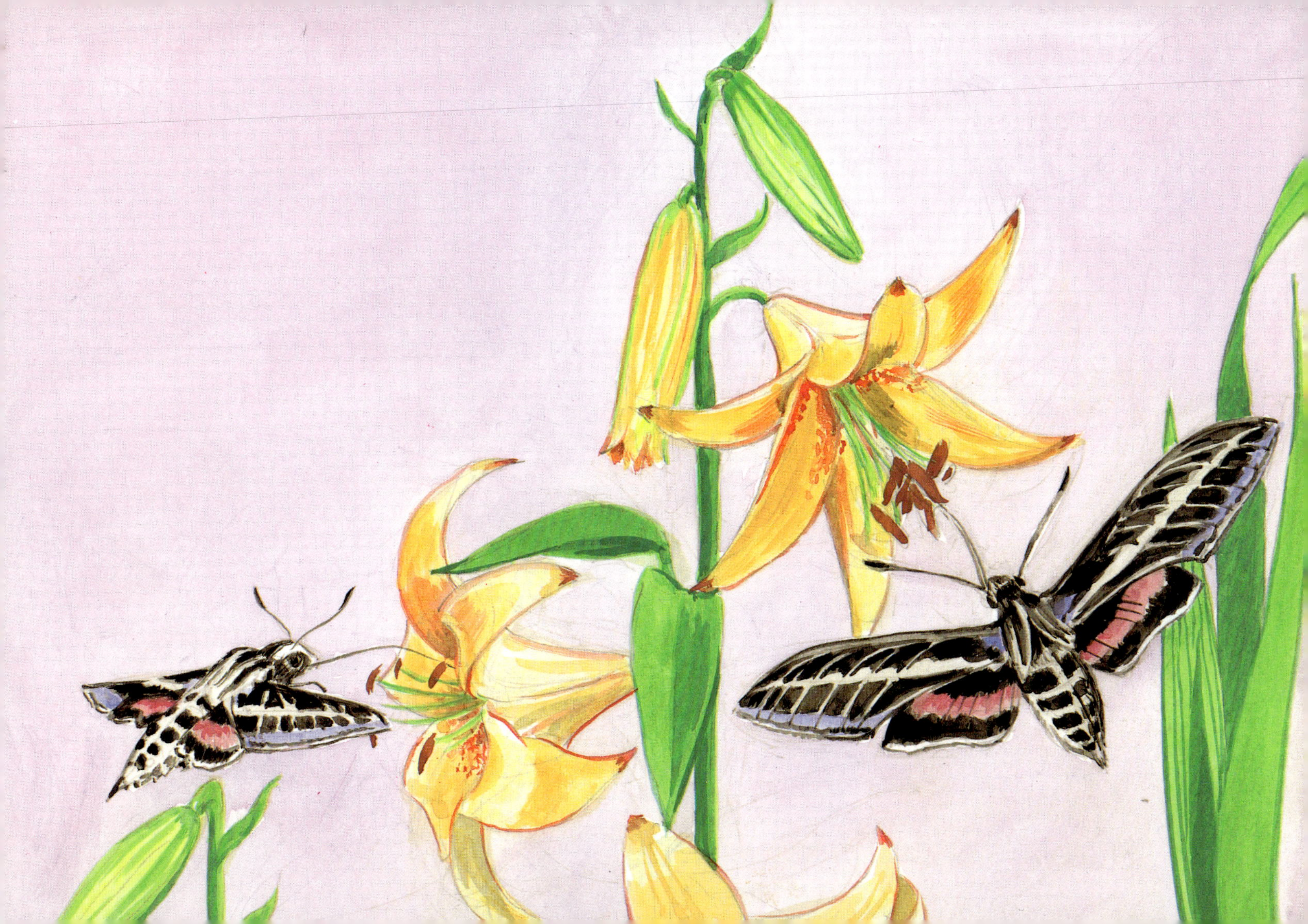

WALKING STICK (10½ CM)

In the fall, walking sticks lay their eggs on the ground. The baby walking sticks hatch in the spring. They shed their skins five or six times before they are full-grown.

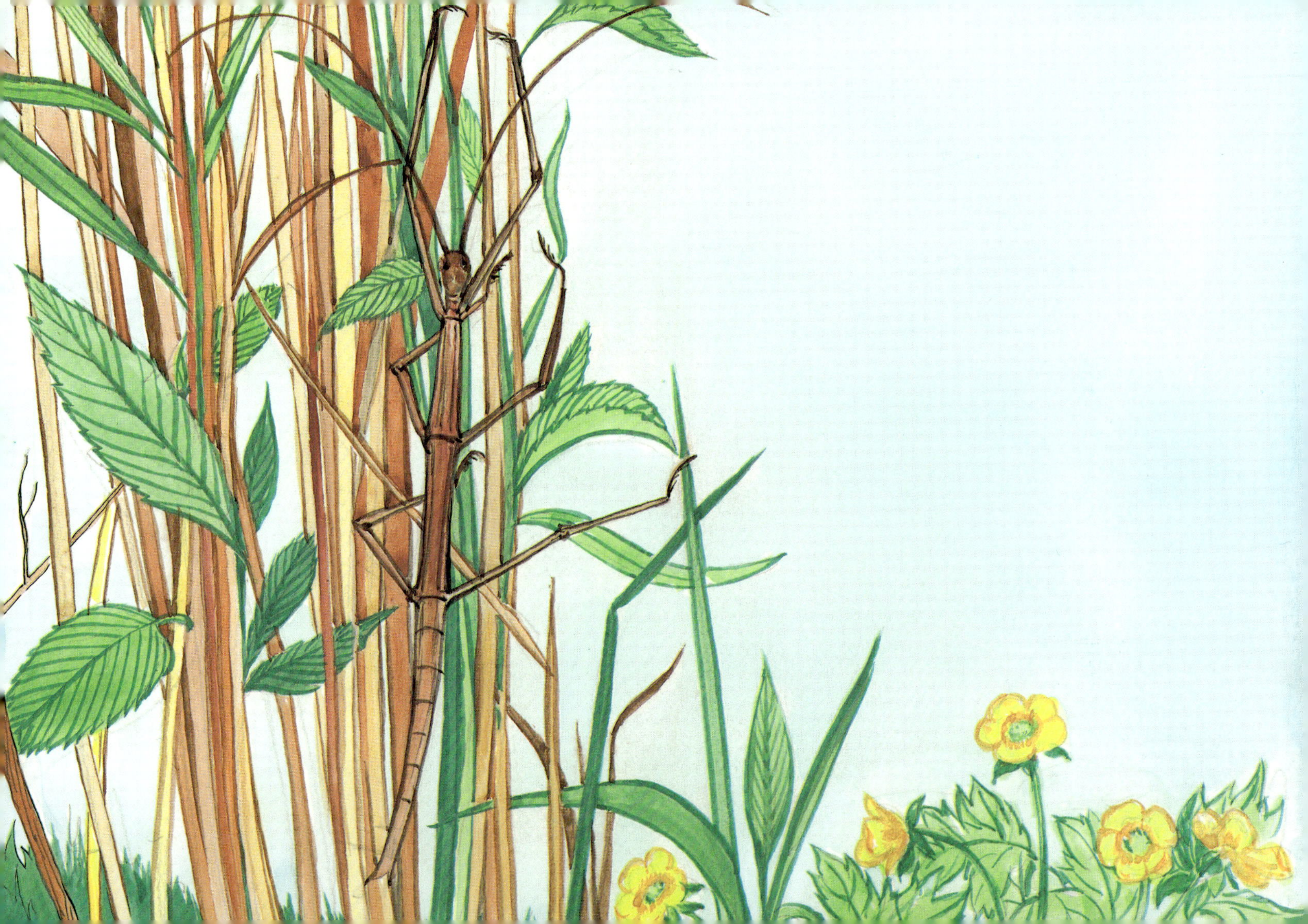

MONARCH BUTTERFLY (10½ CM)

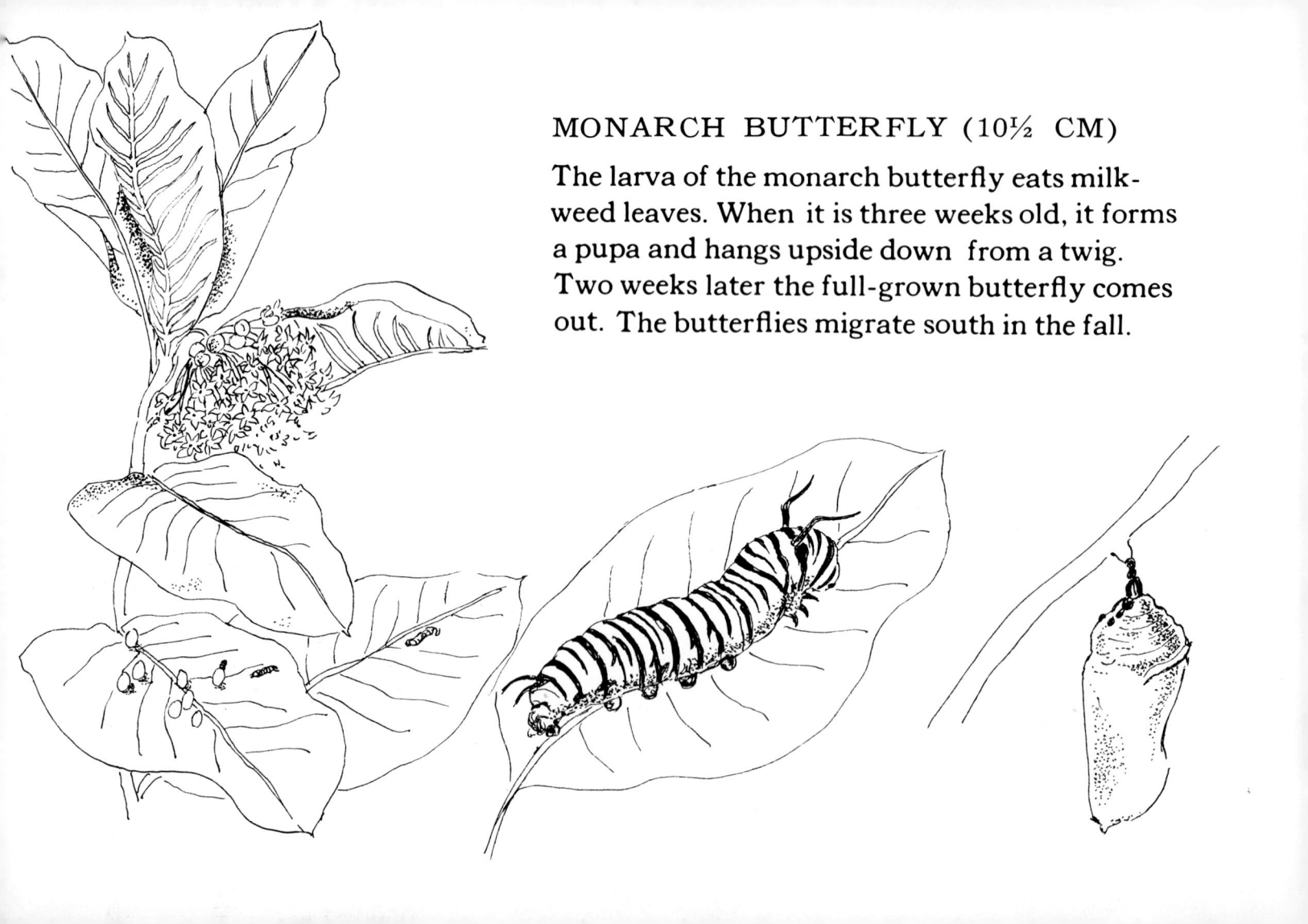

The larva of the monarch butterfly eats milkweed leaves. When it is three weeks old, it forms a pupa and hangs upside down from a twig. Two weeks later the full-grown butterfly comes out. The butterflies migrate south in the fall.

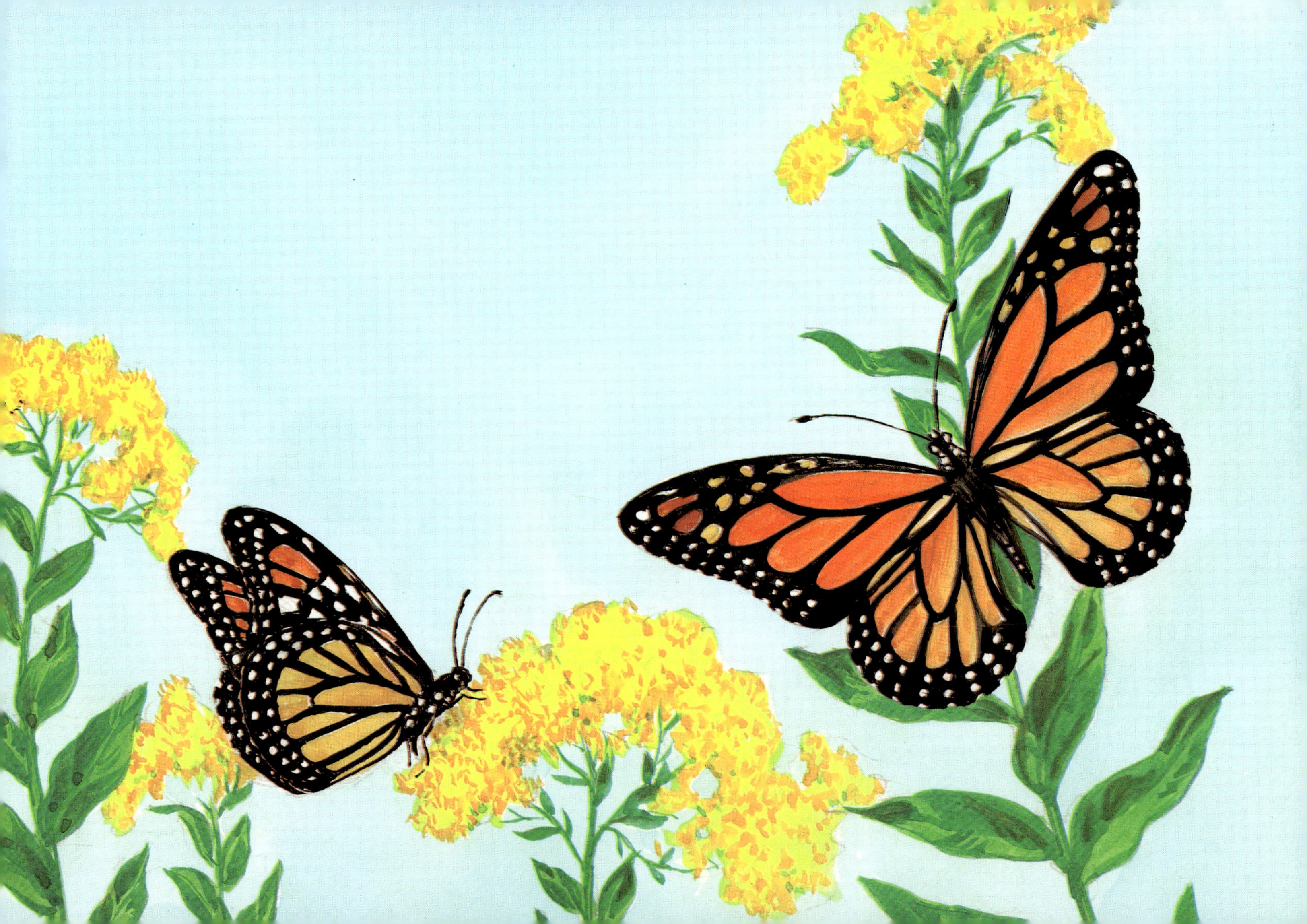

PRAYING MANTIS (11 CM)

The mantis spins a web of silk to hold its eggs. In the spring the eggs hatch. It takes the babies three months to reach their adult size. The praying mantis eats insects that are harmful to plants.

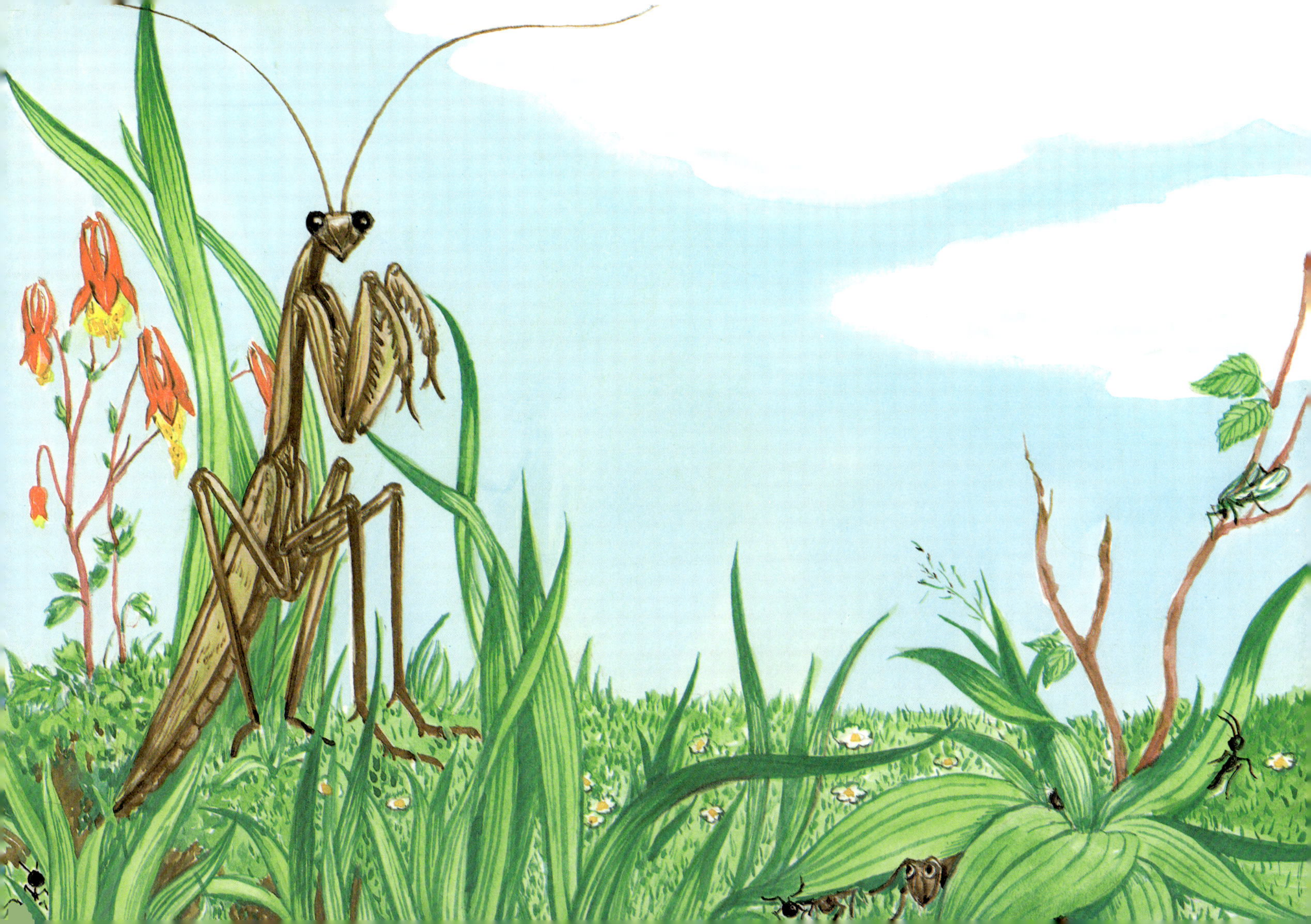

TARANTULA (11 CM)

The mother tarantula carries her eggs in a sac until they hatch. The new babies ride on their mother's back until they are strong enough to walk on their own. Tarantulas can live as long as twenty years.

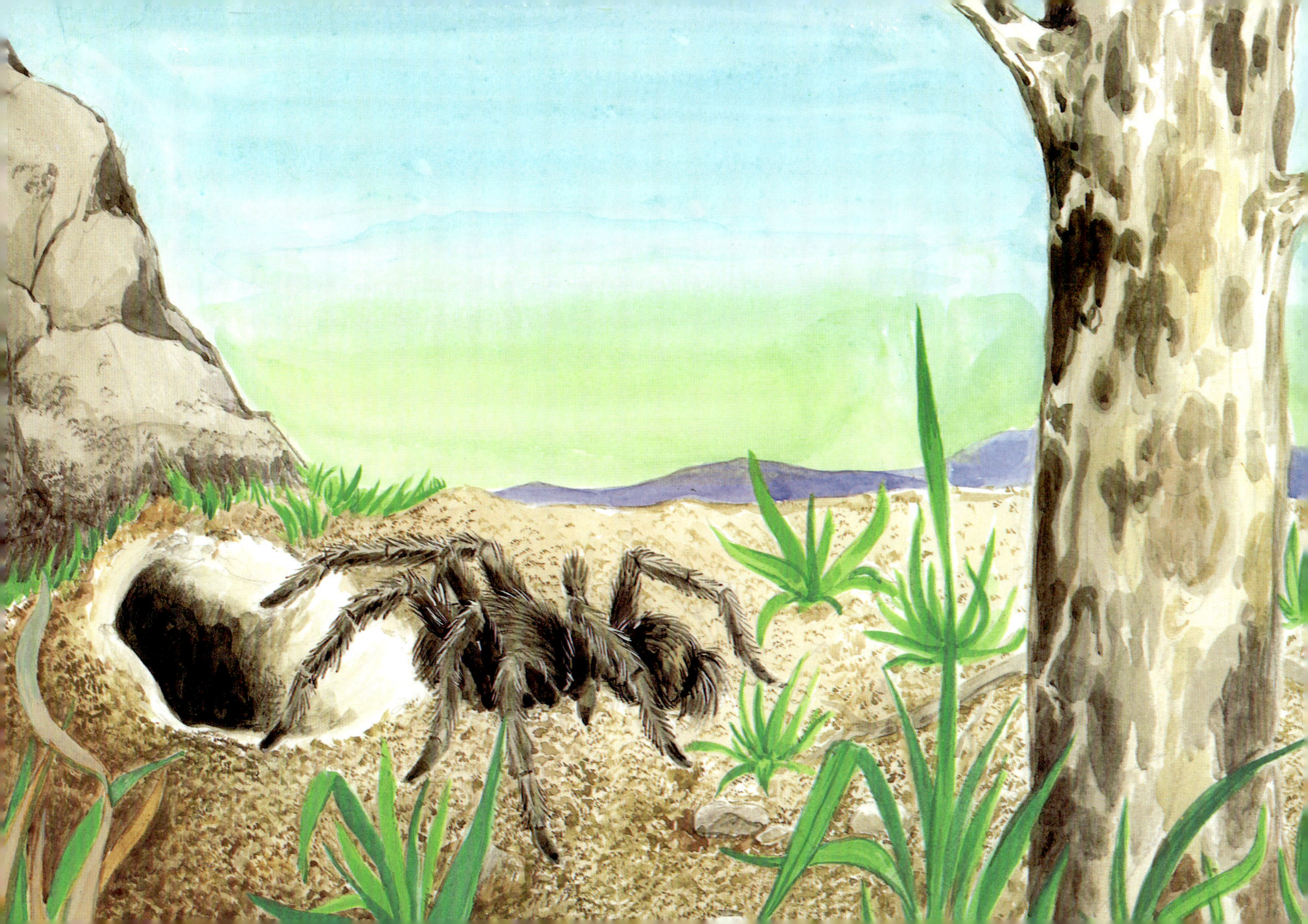

DRAGON FLY (13 CM)

The dragonfly lays its eggs beside a pond. The babies, called nymphs, live in the water. They shed their skin several times as they grow. When they are a year old they crawl out of the water and shed their skin one last time, emerging as full-grown dragonflies.

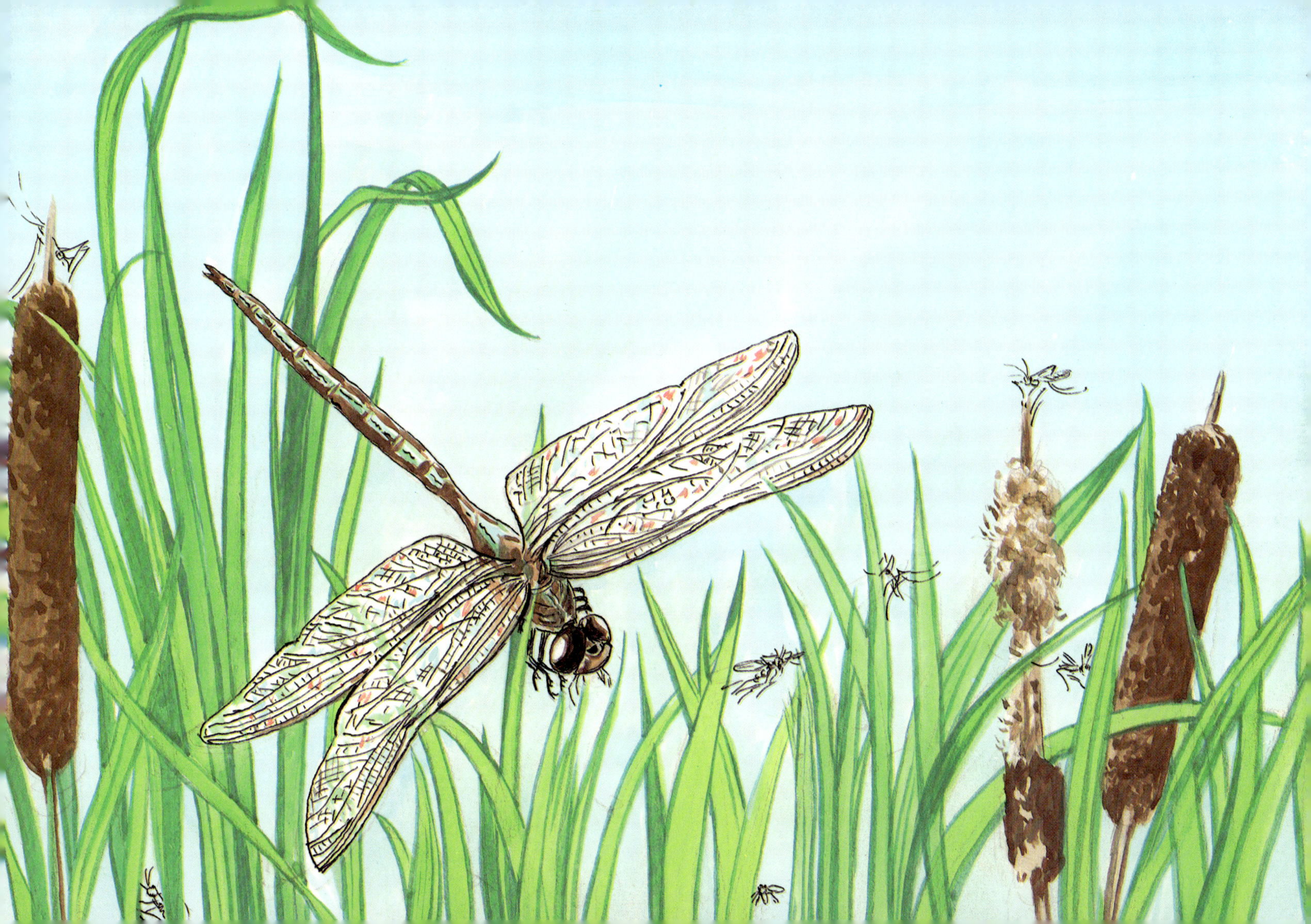

CECROPIA MOTH (Wing Spread 15 CM)

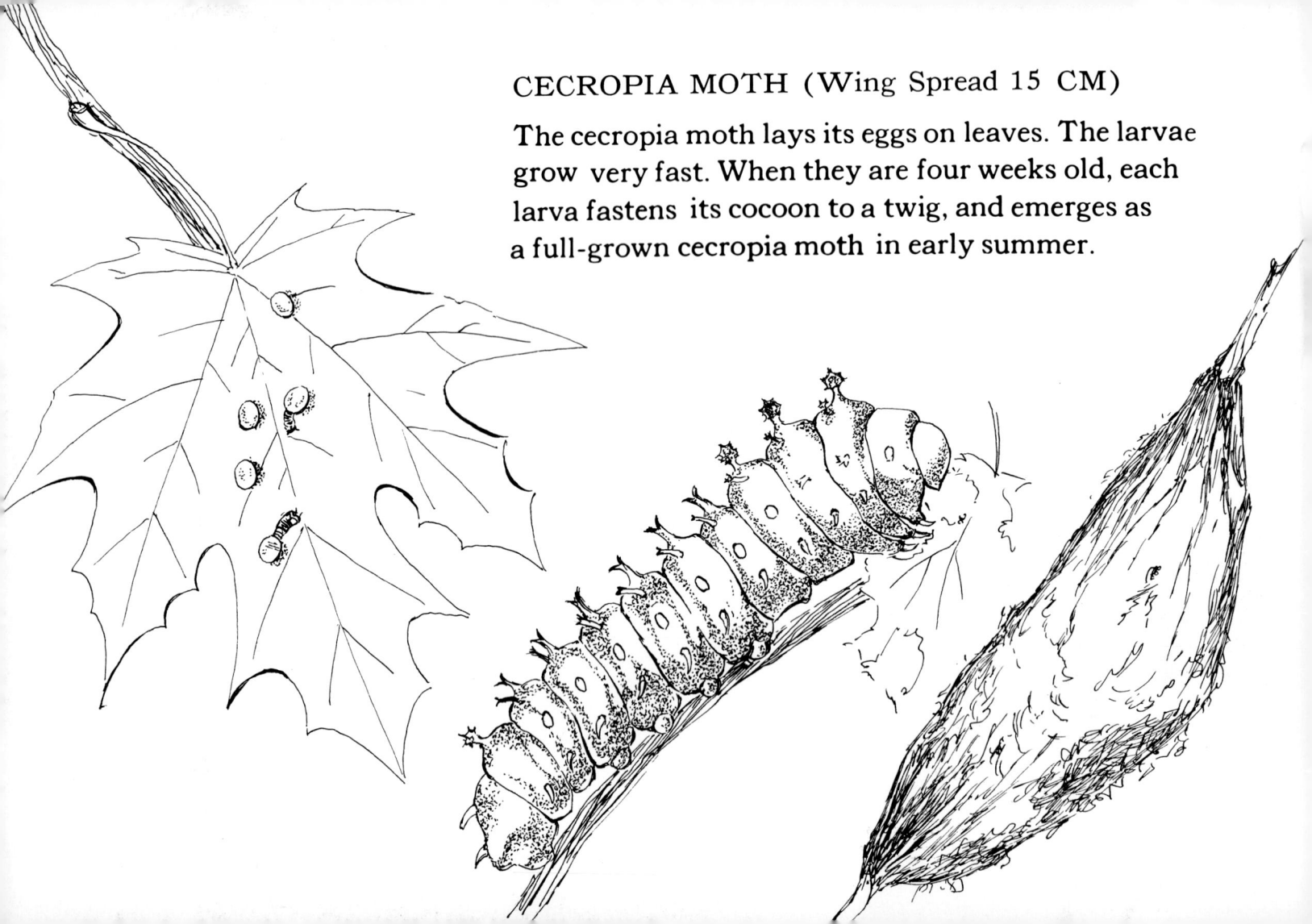

The cecropia moth lays its eggs on leaves. The larvae grow very fast. When they are four weeks old, each larva fastens its cocoon to a twig, and emerges as a full-grown cecropia moth in early summer.

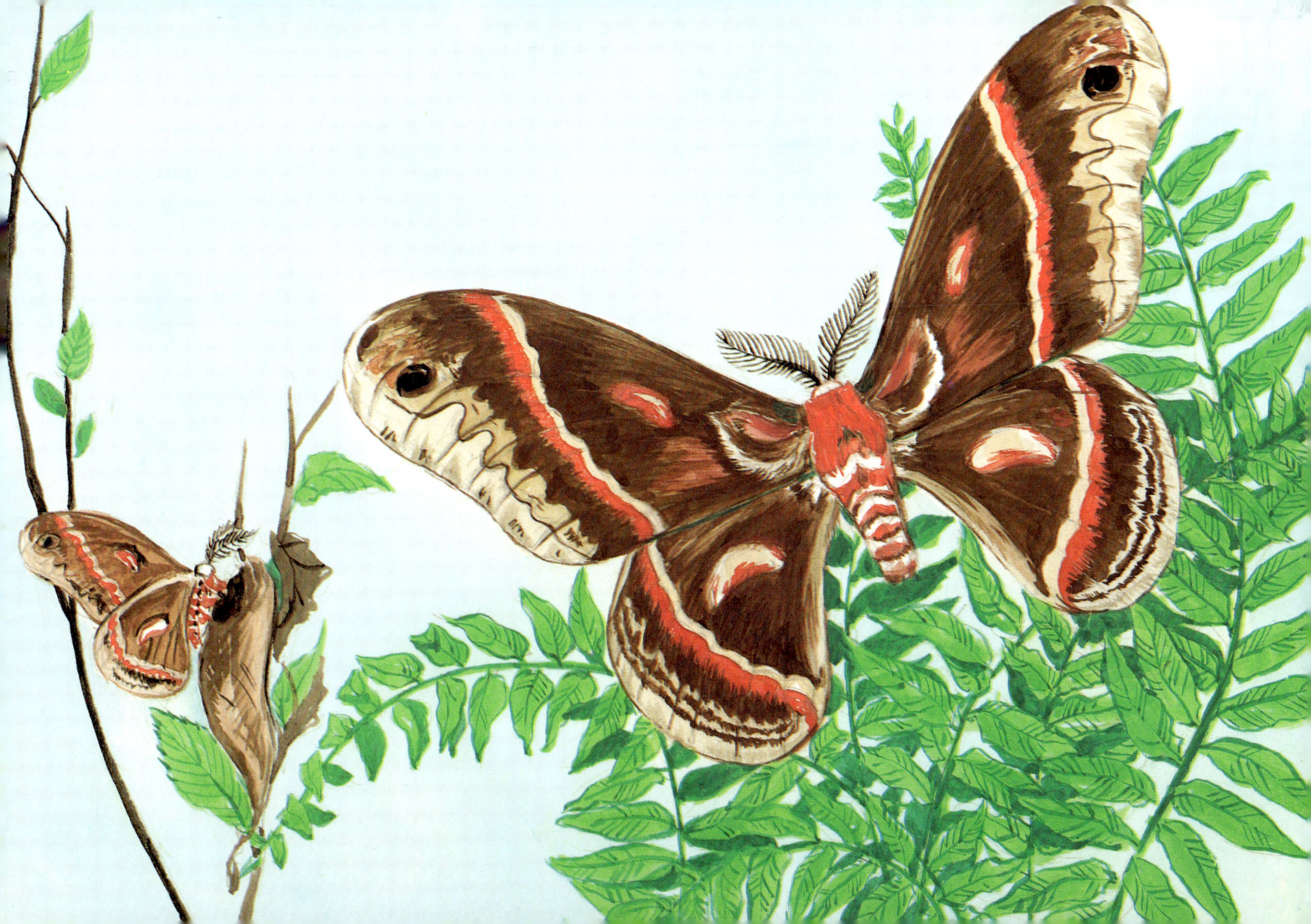

CENTIPEDE (18 CM)

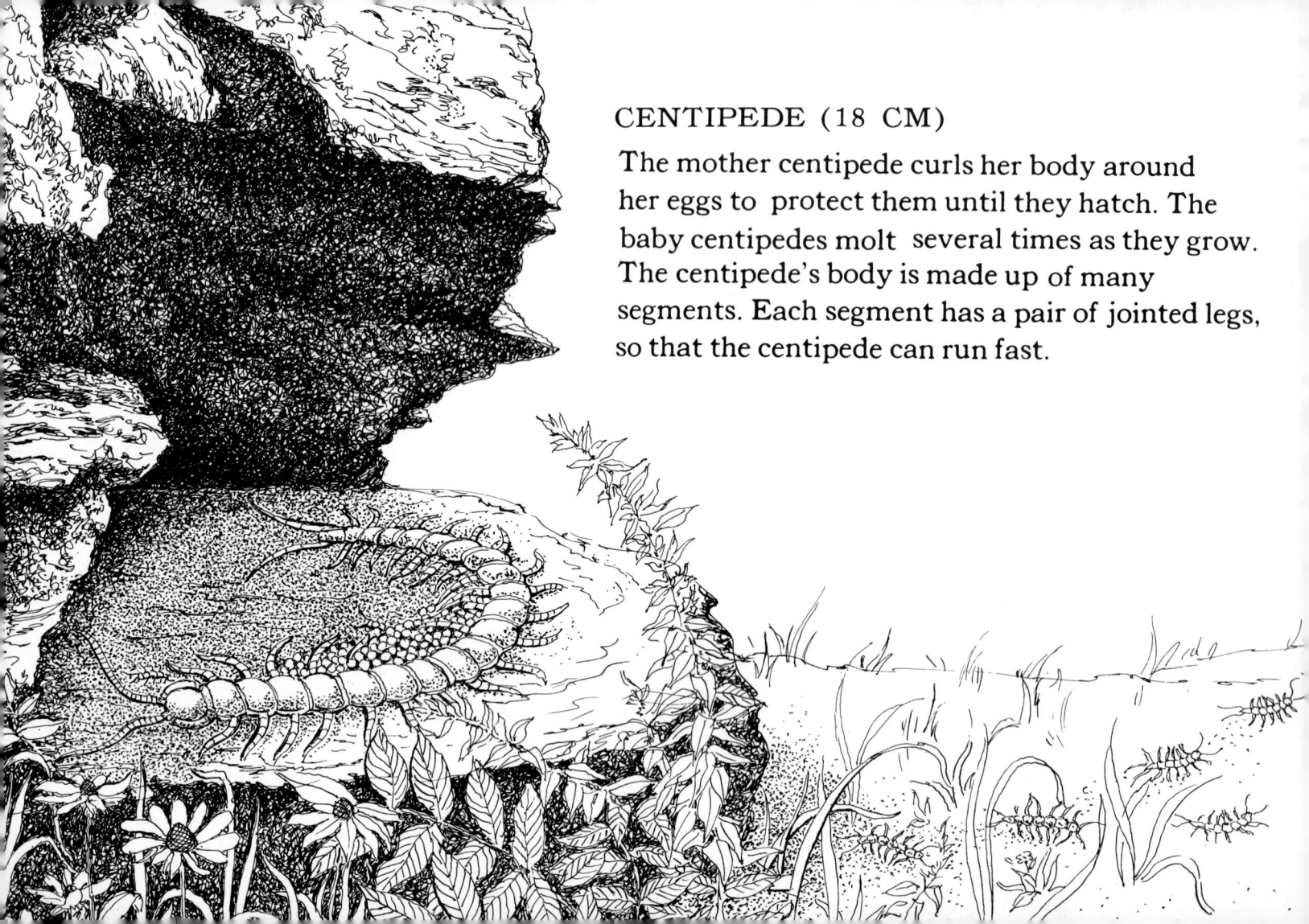

The mother centipede curls her body around her eggs to protect them until they hatch. The baby centipedes molt several times as they grow. The centipede's body is made up of many segments. Each segment has a pair of jointed legs, so that the centipede can run fast.

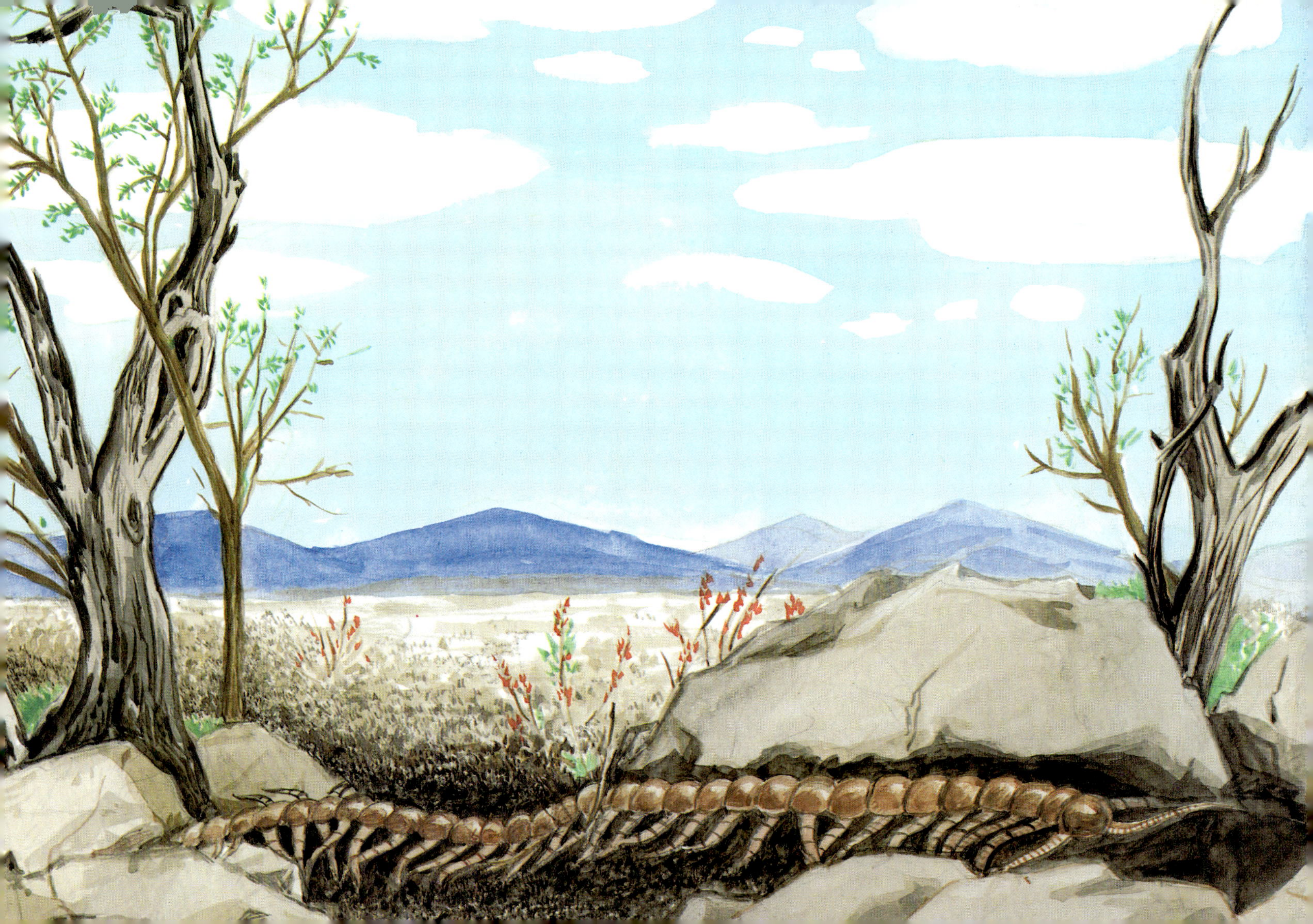

THE EARTHWORM (35 CM)

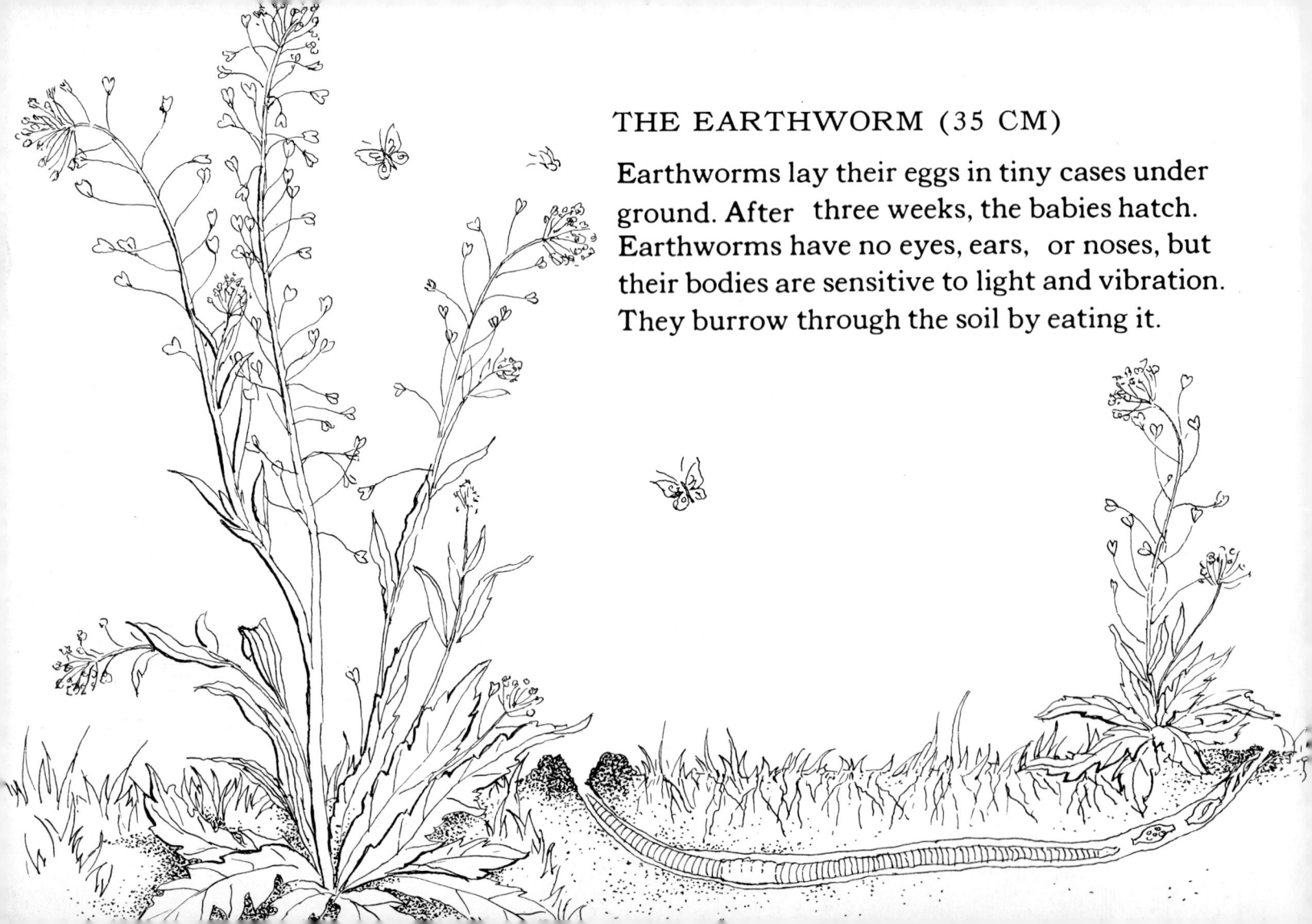

Earthworms lay their eggs in tiny cases under ground. After three weeks, the babies hatch. Earthworms have no eyes, ears, or noses, but their bodies are sensitive to light and vibration. They burrow through the soil by eating it.

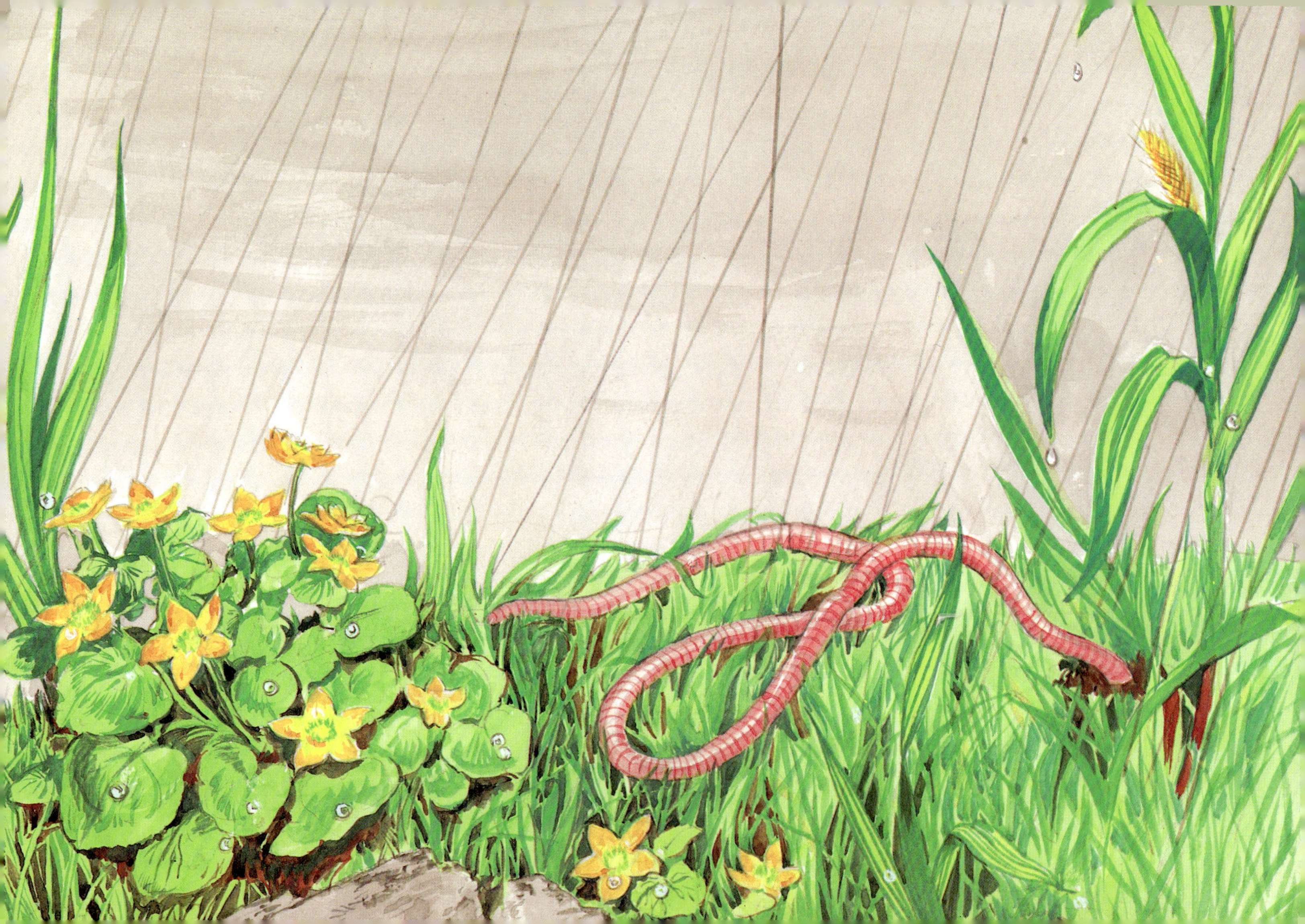

SCALE ½ SIZE   5MM : 1CM

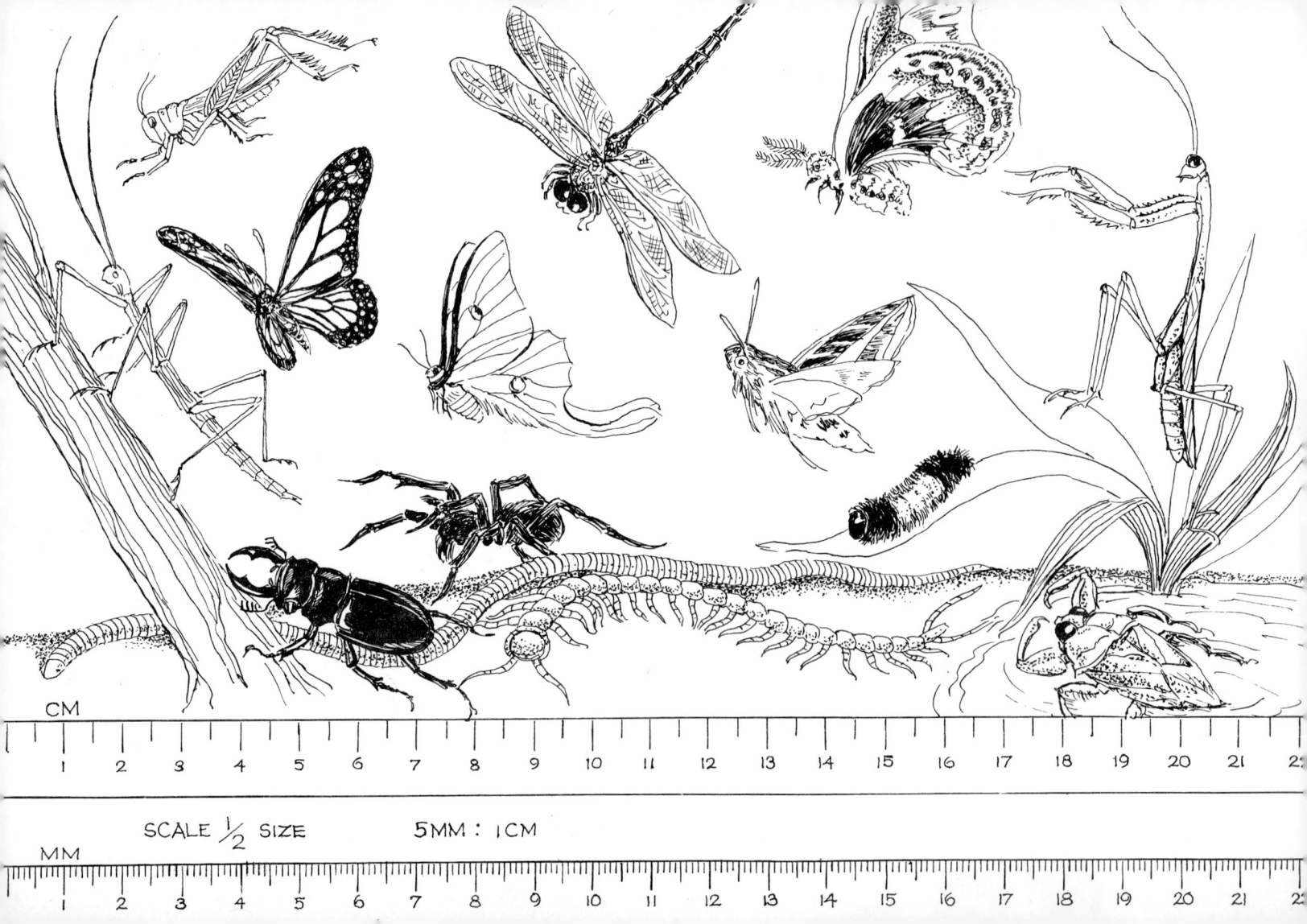